I'll Miss You Later

James W. Gaynor

Copyright© 2021 by James W. Gaynor
All rights reserved
jameswgaynor.com

ISBN 978-0-9978428-4-5 (paperback)
First Edition
Designed by: pak creative, pakcreative.com

For
David Bergman, poet, scholar
and cherished guide
and
remembering always

Panel in The Quilt Project, assembled by Christine Egan and displayed on the National Mall.

Introduction

Prolonged COVID-mandated sheltering in place over the spring and early summer of 2020 gave me the opportunity to start disposing of personal documents that at some point in the relatively near future — I'm now 72 years old — will be of little interest and unnecessary bother to anyone dealing with my papers.

While shredding away, I found a pocket notebook that I kept from 1986 to 1997, during the worst years of the AIDS epidemic in New York City. I kept it separate from my journals, specifically as a help in organizing memorial services (eventually, there were 38). It was also a record of thoughts that cropped up when gathering details of my friends' lives. There were notations and contact information for relatives, newspapers, venues, florists, ministers, rabbis, a rebel Jesuit and a terrific Wiccan priestess — as well as scribbled notes to self, such as "family is Southern Baptist ODG, get rid of porn"; "F. hated sonnets"; "Sondheim again! write something about Into the Woods and urban mythology"; etc., etc., one heartbreaking et cetera after another.

Some of the ideas eventually became poems, a few of which — much later — appeared in print. But finding the notebook, 23 years after its last entry — torn red cover, unwinding wire binding — made me think about going back and putting them together in the chronological order they suggested themselves.

The result is "I'll Miss You Later" — one poem in 20 parts, forged in one epidemic — during an administration that initially did nothing because the initial affected populations were deemed undesirable (i.e., gay, Haitian, drug addicts) — and assembled in another epidemic under an administration that initially did nothing because the initial affected population was deemed non-essential (i.e., old).

Since I'm now both old and gay, I have no idea how I'm still here. But putting these pieces together has made me realize poets and epidemiologists have something in common: love and viruses never disappear completely — and they share the disquieting habit of showing up again when least expected.

— James W. Gaynor
New York City 2020

[1984]

*How did you go bankrupt?" Bill asked.
"Two ways," Mike said. "Gradually, and then
suddenly."*
    — Ernest Hemingway, *The Sun Also Rises*

Our trip took longer than expected
due to stops scheduled and un-
changes in destination and
even though the mirror kept reminding me
objects were closer than they appeared
a warning I chose to disregard
then suddenly I was there

you were not.

[1984]

Reproductive mission accomplished,
the virus finds itself
reduced to shrapnel in the semen
loitering — possibly with intent —
in ejaculate's slippery warmth,
                              which
suggests post-plague reality will require —
in addition to a vaccine — adjectives
worthy of the complexity
now swirling on the tongue,
                          but
a conscious recycling initiative
might better suit the newest normal
a blend of ingredients already on hand, e.g.,

Elegant / Lean   Chewy / Muscular
Nuanced / Airy   Herbaceous / Bold
Delicate / Subtle   Brooding / Pungent
Velvety / Supple Persistent / Flamboyant —

labels borrowed verbatim
from wine-tasting scripts,
                        because
whatever else may change —
word of mouth is a constant.

[1985]

Your memorial service has gathered
an interesting crowd
many with amusing secrets
who have begun to mingle
with the grief and coffee.

Which makes me think
this would be a good time
 to avoid your husband —
 we both know why —
                         and
introduce myself to
the smoldering leather jacket
standing near the door.

I'll miss you later.

[1985]

Absent friends
are the clothes I keep
hoping will come back
into style or at the very least
fit me again.

As once I thought they did.

[1986]

My dream of being a famous jazz harpsichordist
is living somewhere in Brooklyn
in a self-storage unit,
entombed among labeled boxes of
invented memories and sexual fantasies,
stacked on top of a cardboard sarcophagus
containing an unfaithful lover's mummified corpse —
treasures until now undisturbed.

[1987]

Too much of my life too often
has been lived in expectation
acknowledged but more often not
of a dragon
with ruby eyes
an iridescent six-pack
and a dangerous steel-blue Speedo™.

[1988]

Unseen movement heard
sidewinding through the vines
remind me
whenever you weren't here
you were horizontally
entwining in someone else's Eden.

As was I.

[1989]

It's not just a shoelace
but the grief of small things breaking

Together
           we bought the shoes
they went with the suit
the ties the bold striped socks
I wore them in an office life
which like the suit no longer fits
and when we danced
                    together

It's not just a shoelace
but the grief of small things breaking

[1989]

I keep a caged canary —
deep in my darkest mine —
as long as it keeps singing
I like to think I'm safe.

[1989]

PSL for viral epidemics
is characterized by
invisible silver linings
doors slam shut as
windows open and
things happen for a reason,
one of which is
what doesn't kill us
makes us stronger or
at the very least
hasn't killed us yet —
so while everything else
in our lives may be
going all to hell.
it's a good thing we all speak
Platitude as a second language.

[1989]

In winter, the house you left
creaks and shivers at night — like me
a haunted post-war construction
requiring constant upkeep.

Summer sounds, again at night,
are softer — whispers and moans,
regrets in the roofing
given voice by the wind.

Whatever the season,
the house and I guard your secret:
there's a minotaur in the basement, and
when I listen carefully, I hear him.

He's hungry.

[1990]

I'd like to think of this photo
as the last time we were all together
young, healthy, without a clue
but it's more a detailed chart
of who was sleeping with whom.

No, the last time we were all together
was the following summer,
somewhere none of us had been before.
Cell phones weren't yet a thing
and no one brought a camera.

[1990]

We left the bed unmade
and so much more unsaid
all I can do now
is buy new sheets you'd hate
and plow ahead
find another bed.

And while I'm at it
pornographic towels.

[1990]

In your present absence
we have all agreed
to eat crustless sandwiches

that the dog won't miss you
as much as will the cat

and —despite repeated denials in print —
you were Chapter 6 in your
therapist's best-selling *Impossible Patients*.

[1991]

Halloween isn't what it was.

Bedsheet ghosts can still be bribed
to go haunt the neighbors
but when your own phantoms appear
an invisible few you know who
they never stop talking

about what should have
been different despite now
knowing their lives could
only have been what they were
which is why they're dead
and you're not.

October 31st may not be what it was
but there's still the chocolate.

[1992]

Anyone lucky enough to be old
should carry a cane
elegant with a dragonhead handle
and hardened beechwood shaft
a sign of the dangers
of staying alive.

[1993]

Subject Line: Condolence email template

[NAME] is now living in our thoughts, among all of our dear — a few not quite so — departed.

But even spiritual arenas have a maximum capacity and not all of this crowd got along with each other when they were here (you know who I mean).

So, let's be sad but agree to keep only the living in our thoughts and forget [NAME] immediately.

Sincerely,
[YOUR NAME]

[1994]

RIP @leatherwriternyc
mirrored-sunglass companion
explorer of labyrinths
I was you you were me

The tattoos remain as do a few
emotional (and other) scars
but everything else —
folders, pics, passwords —
is headed to the recycle bin.

Yes, I will miss you
our better body
the playground on which
we played so well and so often
with others.

I was you you were me
so much forgotten
now in need of recall
RIP @leatherwriternyc.

[1995]

I miss that moment
we admit we're lost
getting out of the car
unfolding the map
deciding where an
exit was missed
the wrong turn taken.

I miss finding out
where we are now
which is not where
we were going then
how to get there
getting there only to
wonder now what

[1995]

As the designated porn collector
I was a one-man special ops team
going in ahead of the family
with a map of where to look for what

And now — call me Ishmael
because there's no one left
for me to ask —
to whom it may concern:

> *If you're reading this*
> *you've figured out my password*
> *and met those special friends*
> *about whom I never talked.*

> *Please think of them as*
> *minimally dressed mourners*
> *enlivening the funeral and*
> *reading of the will.*

> *And yes there are a few*
> *favorites in the group who*
> *deserve special recognition*
> *for their years of faithful service.*

> *I'm sure you'll be able to cope.*

The author in 1987
Photo: Bill Pierce

About the Author

James W. Gaynor is now working on surviving the third global pandemic of his lifetime. He's the author of *20 Poems About Love + Marriage Inappropriate 4 Weddings, 20 Poems About Life + Death Inappropriate 4 Funerals, 20 Poems 4 Breaking Up Online,* and *Jane Austen's Pride and Prejudice in 61 Haiku.*

More books by James W. Gaynor

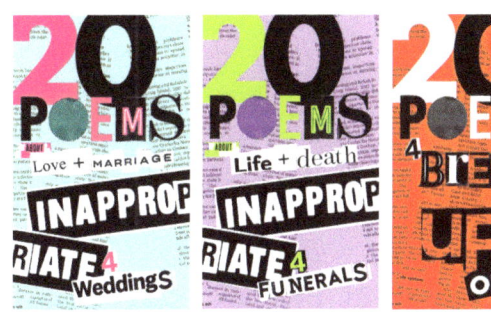

The 20 Poems ebook Series!

❶ 20 Poems About Love + Marriage
  Inappropriate 4 Weddings

❷ 20 Poems About Life + Death
  Inappropriate 4 Funerals

❸ 20 Poems for Breaking Up Online

available at

Jane Austen's Pride and Prejudice in 61 Haiku (1,037 Syllables!)

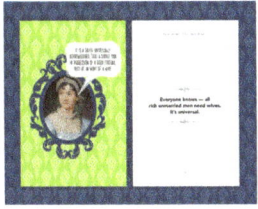

Available at all major booksellers, including Amazon, Barnes & Noble, and independent booksellers nationwide!